BUSINESS IDEAS
TO MAKE A
Million Dollars

BUSINESS IDEAS
TO MAKE A
Million Dollars

Book 2

Joyce Shearin

Trafford rev. 11/02/2011

 www.trafford.com

North America & International
toll-free: 1 888 232 4444 (USA & Canada)
phone: 250 383 6864 ♦ fax: 812 355 4082

All Business Ideas To Start
(Please Obtain Needed Permission)

Business To Start:

- Weavelwigs made in America.

- Adjustable size ivory teeth sold over the counter for humans/people.

- Prescription contacts and prefilled eyeglasses. Prescriptions over the counter.

- Open a self service mobile vendor snack cart or self service.

- Liquid dental mouthwash.

- Open a karaoke internet café.

- Build premade small homes below current price.

- Start neighborhood bingo community casino.

- GED Book with Diploma in back—$50.00

- Digital Reader ink pens that scan fax and email to places.

- Develop a college degree book with degree in back for non essential issues/professions.

- Automated phoneline for coupons to be mailed to your home.

- Start your own paper magazine.

- Sell fold up purses/pocketbooks.

- Self service DVD purchase counter.

- Flameless state/country adventure vanilla or other scented candles.

- Develop sneaker boots or sneakers with socks attached.

- Calendar bags.

- A professional book with certificate at the back for certain professions that are possible to be done in this city. DVD/CD optional i.e. tap dance, etc.

- Start a messenger/delivery service in your area.

- Start your own fashion collection

- Start your own small farm.

- Open your own small grocery store. Be nice, be good.

- Develop your own school.

- Start an actor's/extra association to get movies done on your own or elsewhere.

- Sell prepackaged popcorn.

- Sell baseballs/all around balls.

- Grocery/ restaurant self service use debit cards/cash machines for checkout.

- Sell voice technology printers.

- Make/develop/sell business plans.

- Develop flu patch sold over the counter with no prescription/ doctor, nurse or pharmacist not needed.

- Develop scanner for teeth with printer capability attached or close.

- Make wine scotch liquids.

- Develop DVD same day movie release production service legally/ legitimately.

- Develop an automated sales line

- Develop water irrigation systems needed in countries like Africa, etc.

- Develop a car with latch at the bottom to walk with options.

- Try to make/growbell/develop anything imported cheaper thru an undercut, i.e. anything made overseas go to made in U.S.A. or locally.

- Develop alternate sources of energy, communication, power, food, housing.

- Always use a prepaid debit card or small cash when possible.

- Automated newspaper dispenser.

- Make anything legal cheaper, that's safe to manufacture.

- Develop a DVD, CD, book with certificate for a defensive driving course to get credit on licenses for driving in addition to the internet for safe driving as well.

- Start your own school.

- Start a neighborhood consignment/ pawnshop.

- Become a cheap car dealer by automated phone, fax, online or in person.

- Develop home cars. Cars that you can live in sometime if possible.

- Develop a lawyer by mail correspondence course if you can get the authorization with diploma at the back or just mail it. (I would be interested, please contact directly at 347-410-7480 if done)

- Develop an optician, doctor or dentist by mail correspondence course with diploma at the back or to be mailed. (I would be interested, please contact directly at 347-410-7480 if done)

- Do a website that prints a family tree individual/person enters data.

- Business plan website, automated phone generation, fax, mail.

- A security police contract.

- Debt clearance company

- Develop an alternative to our current light/gas/cable system besides what we already have. Direct purchase, no billing and affordable.

- Develop a cheap home building company for small homes to be built for land use. Maybe relocated to parks and other sites.

- Become a doctor/dentist or lawyer/doctor.

- Bringing penicillin and steroids over the counter with proper warning labels if possible.

- Set up an account to do money orders.

- Open a 50 cents store for every item.

- Work as many jobs as possible.

- Become a realtor.

- Dried powder soda gingerale, cola, etc.

- Private GED (General high school universal diploma) or develop your own school.

- Do a phone/voice printing system.

- Do a home DNA test kit for genes.

- Do bottled vinegar water/apple vinegar, etc. (helps health and can make money too)

- Develop instant IV pack finger stick with finger holder, if possible.

- Make a wheelchair access/handicap disability small cars.

- Apartment cleaning system.

- Develop a relay phone that prints and reads your voice for over the counter sales.

- Design your own fragrance.

- Develop low on the ground/ floor jeep cars.

- Do a new game for building golf, etc.

- Develop water irrigation systems for dry states like Texas, countries like Africa or do a bottled water brand.

- Develop a scanner that types what is scanned.

- Light steroids sold over the counter. Consumer warning and responsibility disclaimer on product.

- Make stuffed animals/toys.

- Start an online magazine.

- Start an online tax prep program that runs itself

- Sell emergency kits.

- Sell fire extinguishers.

- Sell anything undercut(cheaper)

- Work harder (health provided)

- See if you can offer a cheaper government service.

- Make small cheap battery operated blenders with cup cover.

- Develop 911 call walkie talkies for people. Registered walkie talkies that can radio 911 and talk for emergency personnel or people.

- Lollipop cakes—sticks with small circle cakes on them.

- Develop independent private self serve mailing box outlets with stamps/ money orders/ boxes.

- Grocery delivery service (Be good, reliable, reputable and fast in this business)

- Make finger balloons, use gloves.

- Develop CD walkman with radio

- Develop an American taxicab company

- Make finger balloons, use gloves.

STAY ACTIVE

STAY INVOLVED

OBEY THE LAW

START A LITTLE SPORTS TEAM
TO STAY IN SHAPE

BE KIND

THANK YOU

www.ingramcontent.com/pod-product-compliance
Lightning Source LLC
Chambersburg PA
CBHW070232290526
45789CB00004B/1585